CELTIC
MANDALAS

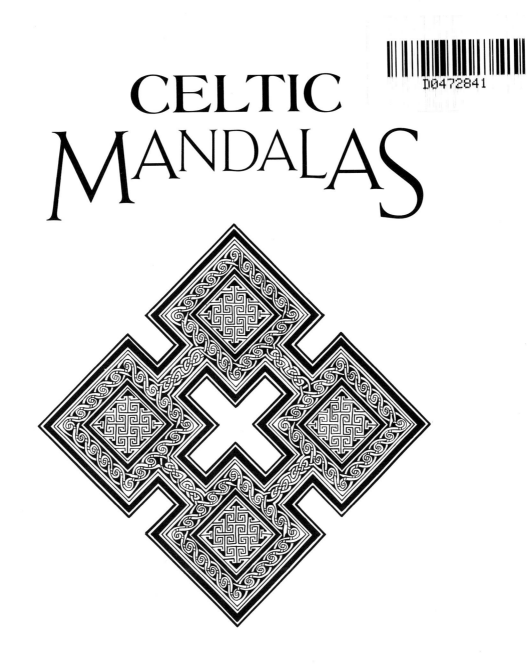

CELTIC
MANDALAS

COURTNEY DAVIS
Text by Helena Paterson

BLANDFORD

ExLibris

A BLANDFORD BOOK
First published in the UK
by Blandford
A Cassell imprint
Villiers House, 41/47 Strand, London WC2N 5JE

Distributed in the United States by Sterling Publishing Co., Inc.
387 Park Avenue South, New York, NY 10016-8810

Distributed in Australia by Capricorn Link (Australia) Pty Ltd
2/13 Carrington Road, Castle Hill, NSW 2154

British Library Cataloguing-in-Publication Data
A catalogue entry for this title is available from the British Library

ISBN 0-7137-2389-0
(Paperback)

Designed by Richard Carr
Typeset by Litho Link Ltd, Welshpool, Powys, Wales
Printed and bound in Spain

contents

The Sacred Thread ✦ Dedicated to my mother and Father and the Sacred Thread

acknowledgements

I cannot thank Helena Paterson enough for the hard work she has put into this book. As always, she is a real inspiration.

Thanks also to Dimity, who amazingly calms me through my frustrations when pen and paper are flying.

Thanks to the Sacred Thread that binds us all, past and present, and to those other bright souls I have walked beside on my journey.

May their lights always shine.

introduction

MANDALAS REPRESENT the magical symbolism of the universe as perceived by ourselves, its intricate construction being contained within the 'eternal circle', which in the East represented the Wheel of Life. People's role or quest was to follow the unbroken thread along a pathway that led ultimately to divine union with a universal Creator or Creatrix.

Most major religions have mandalas. Ancient Egyptian priests invented mysterious hieroglyphs based upon all the names of their deities which, when spoken, granted the earthbound soul direct access to Heaven. The ancient Greeks, who were brilliant mathematicians, perceived the universe and mankind in the form of sacred geometry: a formula interpreted through their astrology as a symbolic language of cosmology. Tibetan Buddhist monks constructed elaborate mandalas that represented the illusion of earthly life, a belief central to their karmic philosophy. Meanwhile, Christian monks incorporated their mandalas into the beautiful stained-glassed windows in their churches and cathedrals, the most famous being the North Rose Window of Chartres Cathedral in France. Likewise, Muslim mosques are decorated with exquisite mosaics.

Celtic mandalas are intricate compositions which invariably have a dual-dimensional format, relating to the belief that it is possible to travel from the earthly realm into the Celtic Otherworld. These two realms represent the ascent and descent of the soul on the Golden Wheel of Life, which refers to the Druidic belief in reincarnation. In Christianity this spiritual 'revolution' was associated with the prospect of Heaven and Hell; and as the Celts' spiritual nature evolved through Christian concepts, this journey became identified with the Quest of the Holy Grail.

Courtney Davis has revised and reconstructed the classic art of the Celts and, in doing so, has rediscovered a 'time tunnel' into the Celtic Otherworld. Colour is a variation of light; a visual sensation and perception. The Celtic perception of colour was vividly dynamic, and has been translated by Courtney with stunning visual effect in his mandalas.

The 'meditative' mandalas have an evocative symbolism, while the 'magical' mandalas provide a key to a Western mystery tradition, an ancient ancestral wisdom which is perhaps so relevant to New Age ideology. The 'astrological' mandalas relate to the twelve zodiac constellations observed by the Druids, who incorporated the signs into their ritual Tree Calendar. This particular imagery is powerfully interpreted by Courtney and provides a source book of Celtic archetypal gods and goddesses.

CLASSIC VERSE

Wherever the fates, in their ebb and flow, lead us – let us follow.

Virgil

the mandalas

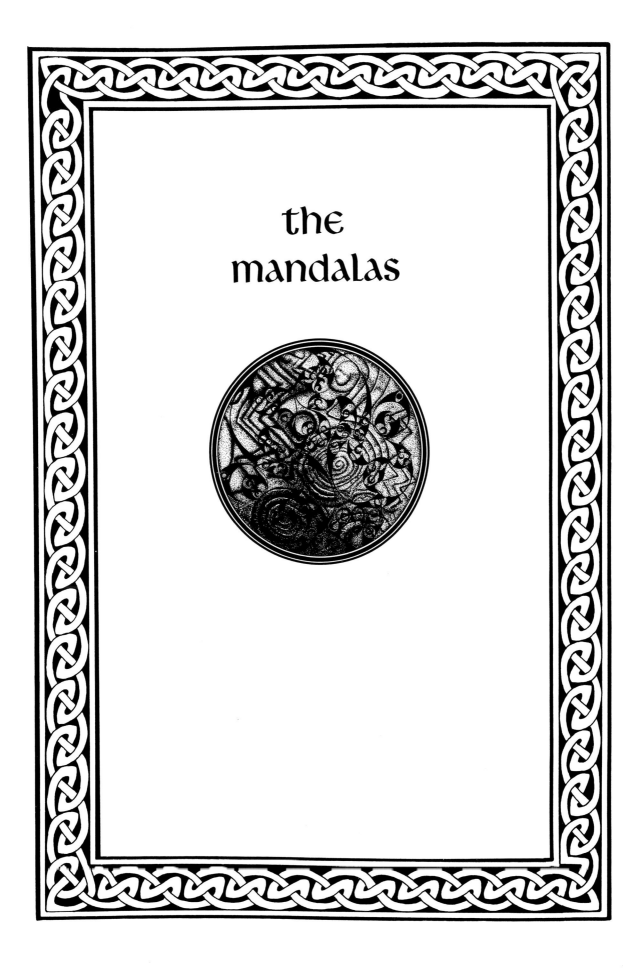

TREE DRYADS

Tree dryads or spirits were believed, according to the Druids, to have been created through the first rays of the Sun that had reached Earth long before human beings appeared. With their help, people were said to have been created, and they represent the spiritual agents or mediators of an invisible Creator or Creatrix. Without trees, the atmosphere on Earth would revert to becoming poisonous for human beings. The magical symbolism of this mandala reflects this life-giving energy.

THE CIRCLE OF GWYNVYD

The Circle of Gwynvyd – cosmic symbol of the Sun and a Circle of Creation that all Celts aspired to reach. It represented a place of the evolved spirit, which became accessible at the time of the solstices. This pathway may be a profound experience for those seeking reunion with their Higher Self. As a meditative glyph, the inspiring beauty and harmony of the cosmos is revealed. When earthly life has reached a degree of fulfilment, evoke the ultimate destiny of the Circle of Gwynvyd.

'THE STRANGE COUNTRY'

I have come from a Land of Light
To a Strange Country;
The Land I have left is forgotten quite
In the Land I see.

The round Earth rolls beneath my feet,
And the still Stars glow,
The murmuring Waters rise and retreat,
The Winds come and go.

Robert Buchanan

BLUE STAR

The lovely blue star Vega was closely observed by Celtic mariners as a location marker of the pole star, which determined their northerly direction. They also believed that Vega controlled the seas, in unison with the Moon. In Druidic cosmology, Vega was an important star, associated with five stages or spheres of Primal Creation: three were outer spheres and two were Earth spheres – comprising land and sea. The magical symbolism of this mandala reflects the magnitude of their vision.

EVOLVING SPIRIT

The Evolving Spirit – symbol of divine love which unfolds like a beautiful flower. This exquisite mandala radiates a healing light from the heart or central spiral. The elaborate design sparkles like a well-cut gem, each facet a reflection of a perfect stone. This pathway has a simple message of love which generates a renewal of faith in a divine purpose for humanity. As a meditative glyph, the imagery flows quietly like a rippling stream. When life energy is 'becalmed', evoke the mystical impetus of the Evolving Spirit.

'TREBARROW'

Did the wild blast of battle sound,
Of old, from yonder lonely mound?
Race of Pendragon! did ye pour,
On this dear earth, your votive gore?

The wayward winds no answer breathe,
No legend cometh from beneath,
Of chief, with good sword at his side,
Or Druid in his tomb of pride.

Stephen Hawker

'HYMN TO COLOUR'

Shall man into the mystery of breath,
From his quick breathing pulse a pathway spy?
Or learn the secret of the shrouded death,
By lifting up the lid of a white eye?

George Meredith

STAR SPIRALS

Star spirals form the pattern of our universe and countless universes beyond our world. Spiral decorations are even more ancient than key patterns, and the most beautiful natural example here on Earth is the nautilus shell. Australian Aboriginals believe it to be the skeletal soul of their Moon God, Alinda, who falls into the ocean every lunar month. Spiral symbols deorate Newgrange, the megalithic earth tomb in Ireland. The magical symbolism reflects the spiralling energy of the universe.

'ODE TO MUSIC'

Man born of desire
Cometh out of the night,
A wandering spark of fire,
A lonely word of eternal thought
Echoing in chance and forgot.

Robert Bridges

KNOTWORK PATTERNS

Knotwork – symbol of continuity. This mandala represents the artistry of Pictish designs; a three-dimensional aspect of Creation. It recalls the enchantment of a bygone age when the pre-Celtic Pictish craftsmen evoked their ancestral spirits for guidance and inspiration. This pathway may be most instructive to those seeking ancestral roots. As a meditative glyph, it encourages a sense of personal identity and awareness. When life becomes a dull, repetitive routine, evoke the ancestral spirits of the Picts.

'THE SORROW OF DELIGHT'

Till death be filled with darkness
And life be filled with light,
The sorrow of ancient sorrows
Shall be the Sorrow of Night:
But then the sorrow of sorrows
Shall be the Sorrow of Delight.

Fiona Macleod

THE CELTIC LOVE-KNOT

The Celtic love-knot – symbol of eternal love. The romantic saga of Tristan and Iseult is a classic tale of undying love and the tragic consequences of jealousy which love can unwittingly evoke. The design of this mandala conveys the intimate relationship of lovers, ever united in their dreams. This pathway may confirm whether a bond is forged or likely to end in failure. As a meditative glyph, it will uncover hidden desires. When life has become a trail of broken promises, evoke the Celtic love-knot.

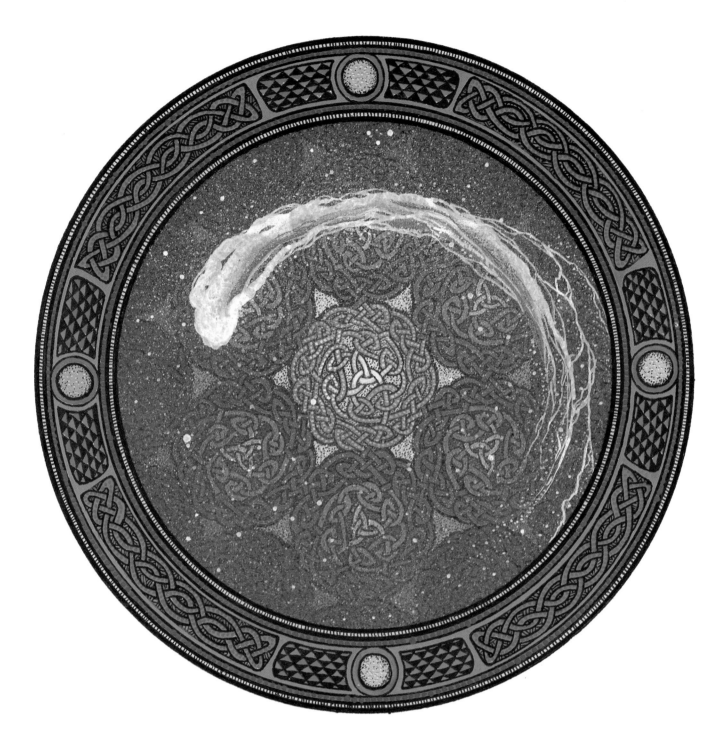

SPIRIT OF ARIANRHOD

The Spirit of Arianrhod – symbol of prophecy and dreams. Arianhod is a mysterious Celtic goddess whose pathway is an eternal quest or thread that has no beginning or end. She controls the time dimension that allows access into the galactic vortex – the whirlpool of Creation; an enigmatic vision of the universe as perceived by the Celts. As a meditative glyph, it provides a glimpse of both the past and the future, but the traveller must follow the Spirit of Arianrhod with an open heart and mind.

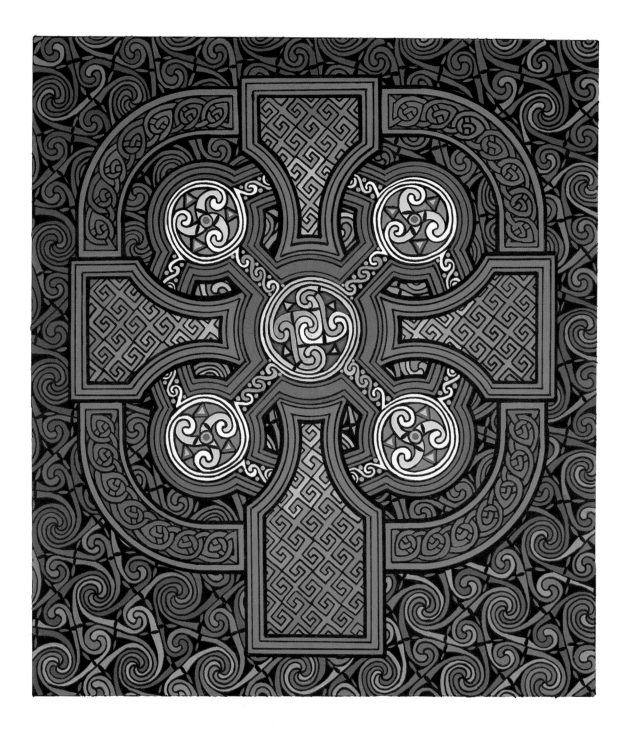

DUAL DIMENSIONS

Dual dimensions – symbol of light and darkness; a polarizing concept of Creation in Celtic myth. Triple spirals form an interconnecting cross, a dual aspect of Christianity as envisaged by the Celts. It reminds the traveller that good and evil can manifest themselves in reverse roles in order to test the integrity of the soul. As a meditative glyph, it activates a subtle transformation of this duality. Thus when life becomes fragmented and a sense of isolation prevails, evoke the Dual-dimensional Cross.

THE CELTIC CROSS

The Celtic Cross — symbol of sacrifice and the promise of eternal life; sentinel of the revolving doorway into Otherworld. A faint glimmer of light beyond this door beckons the weary traveller who seeks solitude and peace of mind. The healing colours of this mandala denote a time for pause and reflection. As a meditative glyph, it opens a door into a crystal pool; the quiet waters that refresh the spirit. Hold fast to this imagery, and when hope fades into dreams that cannot be remembered, evoke the Celtic Cross.

CELTIC TRISKELE

The Celtic triskele originally symbolized a three-dimensional world of Land, Sea and Air. The fourth element, Fire, belonged to the gods. The number 'three' was also the sacred number of their Lunar Goddess, Ceridwen, who presided over the ancient Matriarchal Trinity of Mother, Lover, Son. This mandala depicts this triple aspect of Creation, which became identified with the Druids' Three Circles of Creation. The magical symbolism reflects this ancient Trinity.

THE CIRCLE OF CEUGANT

The Circle of Ceugant – cosmic symbol and a Circle of Creation identified with the Cygnus constellation (the Swan). Its bright star, Deneb, is aligned to most major stone circles in Britain. The evolving centre of spirals depicts the serpentine galaxy in a fiery sea of cosmic energy and light. This pathway may be a difficult one to follow without being blinded by what Cabbalists refer to as 'limitless light'. With this meditative glyph, commence one step at a time. Thus when life has ceased to be a challenge in the learning sense, evoke the cosmic light of Ceugant.

GREEN CRYSTAL

A green crystal or emerald was mounted on the magical scabbard of the sword Excalibur, a gift from the Lady of the Lake to King Arthur. Possession of the scabbard protected the life of the king, for no wound could be inflicted upon him in battle while armed with both the sword and scabbard. When Morgan le Fay stole the scabbard, he succumbed to his fate as sacrificial Sun-king. The magical symbolism of this mandala reflects the spirit of the green crystal – the supernatural realm.

EXTRACT FROM CELTIC ART,
THE METHOD OF CONSTRUCTION,
'THE SPIRAL'

*'The spiral as a symbol and as an ornament had a beginning at
the dawn of man's intellect.'*

George Bain

REVOLVING DOORWAY

The revolving doorway to beyond the universe in Druidic cosmology was associated with Capella, the chief star of the Auriga constellation. The mysterious Lunar Goddess Arianrhod guarded this entrance and is related to the search for immortality, which later became associated with the Quest of the Holy Grail in Arthurian legend. This particular legend is now a universal myth, which confirms the unique influence of Celtic literature. The magical symbolism of this mandala reflects this evolving quest.

KEY PATTERNS

Key patterns were used as a form of decoration on mammoth ivories as early as 20,000 BC and have adorned ancient temples around the world from South America (Mayan civilization) to Greece (Mycenaean period). Key designs also decorated the once magnificent Temple of Solomon. But it was the ancient Picts, who intermarried with the Celts, who perfected the decorative art of key patterns, and the magical symbolism of this Pictish/Celtic design reflects the riddle of the universe.

GOLDEN KEY

A golden key to unlock the secret of the universe perhaps? The Celtic bards composed poems in the form of riddles which required answers. To 'speak in riddles' was their own way of trying to solve the mysteries of life. Time has moved on, but some riddles still remain unanswered, despite the triumph of modern technology. The magical symbolism of this mandala recalls a poem known as the 'Enigma of the Bards'.

EXTRACTS FROM 'THE GAME OF LIFE',
THE WEB OF ENCHANTMENT

Before the 'Fall', before the storm,
And ere our spirits first took form,
There was a Plan, a chequered Game
And we were formed – so we became
The pawns in bodies – on Life's Board.

Clare Marfell-Harris

DREAMTIME

Dreamtime is an out-of-body experience which all ancient people regarded as highly significant and revealing. Primitive people looked up at the distant stars and dreamt of being united with their Creator/Creatrix. A starry sky covers the Earth like a jewel-studded mantle, and has inspired poets and dreamers ever since human beings first walked upon Earth. Dreaming releases the earthbound spirit, and the magical symbolism of this mandala reflects this journey to the stars.

ZOOMORPHIC ARTISTRY

Zoomorphic artistry is based upon abstract forms of animals, birds and reptiles. The curious intertwining expresses the mythical nature and origins of all living things on Earth in the Celtic Tree of Life. The animal kingdom represented a mystical realm in Druidism, a source of life experience that people sometimes returned to in order to regain lost knowledge. The magical symbolism of this mandala reflects this shape-changing process.

SERPENTINE JEWEL

A serpentine jewel refers to a 'snakestone' or 'serpent egg', a magical talisman said to have been formed when snakes intertwined themselves into a ball on a certain day of the Moon. Their secretion and spittle formed a bluish-green substance called 'anguinum', which then crystallized into 'Druid's glass'. The Druids believed the universe had been hatched from two sea-serpent's eggs, and the magical symbolism of this mandala reflects this mystical element of Druidism.

CELTIC IMAGERY

The realm of Celtic imagery is vivid and artistically inspired. It reveals an enlightened form of self-awareness, a powerful sense of individuality that remains the hallmark of Celtic character. This mandala conveys a rich tapestry of Celtic culture and provides a deep insight into the Celtic psyche. Such imagery unlocks the creative talents which often lie dormant. As a meditative glyph, it may awaken these talents. Thus if life has become a burden of material necessity, evoke Celtic imagery.

EXTRACT FROM 'THE HORSES'

Their eyes as brilliant and as wide as night
Gleamed with cruel apocalyptic sight.
Their manes the leaping ire of wind
Lifted with rage invisible and blind.

Edwin Muir

THE EYE OF SARPH

The Eye of Sarph refers to a star-serpent in Druidic cosmology that encircled Earth. Sarph is another name for the Milky Way or the zodiac constellations. The Eye of Sarph was believed to be a fiery comet that periodically darted across the sky to herald the birth of Sun-kings. The zoomorphic and semi-human figures convey a scene of earthly chaos surrounded by a black sky, which recalls the dark period in history prior to the birth of King Arthur. As a meditative glyph, this pathway is full of colourful encounters with archetypal gods and goddesses.

FIVE GRAALS

The Five Graals represent an evolving symbol or concept of eternal life. The first Graal, the Cauldron of Ceridwen, was the source of all life and wisdom – two concepts presided over by the 'third' initiating power of the Goddess. The second, Christianized, Graal in Arthurian legend identified it with the 'chalice' and the initiatory power was the Holy Virgin, the fourth and fifth concepts being 'love' and 'sacrifice'. The magical symbolism of this mandala reflects the elaborate imagery of Celtic vision.

'THOUGHTS ON THE SHAPE
OF THE HUMAN BODY'

How can we find? how can we rest? how can
We, being gods, win joy, or peace, being man?

Rupert Brooke

THE CELTIC TREE OF LIFE

The Celtic Tree of Life — symbol of Creation and the evolving spirit of human beings. The intertwining dragon-flies symbolize the spirit of the Faery people who, in Celtic myth, represented ancestral gods and goddesses. As a meditative glyph, it acts as a connecting link with the invisible life energy which flows through every living creature on Earth. When life energy is at a low ebb and all action appears counter-productive, evoke the well-source of the Celtic Tree of Life.

'THE PAGAN'

Heart of granite, earth and sea –
Soul of old antiquity.

Clare Marfell-Harris

DARK JEWEL

A dark jewel is associated in Celtic myth with the 'witching' hour of midnight, when the Dark Lunar Goddess appeared. An awesome deity in all ancient lunar myths, her radiant beauty was cloaked in darkness and concealed in a prism of light resembling an uncut precious stone. The dark jewel of midnight was believed to be a black pearl, an extremely rare jewel considered more precious than diamonds.

'FEATHERSTONE'S DOOM'

Twist thou and twine! in light and gloom
A spell is on thy hand:
The wind shall be thy changeful loom,
Thy web, the shifting sand.

Stephen Hawker

THE CIRCLE OF ABRED

The Circle of Abred – cosmic symbol of Earth and a Circle of Creation where human beings dwell. Good and evil coexisted in equal measure and influence, and the Druids believed the trial of Abred enabled people finally to ascend to Gwynvyd. The Celtic Cross forms a bridge across the fiery abyss of Annwn, where all earthly life was formed. As a meditative glyph, this pathway may encounter primeval demons that haunt the psyche. But if life has become a trial of unexplained phobias, evoke the purifying fire of Annwn hidden deep within the Circle of Abred.

GOVANNAN'S FIRE

The Celts were greatly skilled in the art of enamelling – the fusion of glass and metal used mainly as an adornment on jewellery. The vibrant colours and design of this mandala recall their artistry as smiths, and their Smith God, Govannan, resembles the Roman god Vulcan or the Greek Hephaestus. Govannan, like all smith gods, was also closely associated with 'initiation' ceremonies which 'freed' the spirit. The magical symbolism of this mandala reflects the source or origin of light born from a primeval darkness.

based on a carving on a granite pillar (1st century BC)

Anglo-Saxon mount (9th century)

THE SERPENT'S STONE

The Serpent's Stone – symbol of an ancient wisdom and fidelity; touchstone of universal truths. The complexity of earthly life sometimes obscures a simple truth. The four serpent heads emerge from the labyrinth of Creation to point the way through self-examination. The brilliant colours convey a sense of drama and intrigue. As a meditative glyph, it endorses the need for self-determination. Thus when truth becomes entangled in a moral dilemma, evoke the secret wisdom of the Serpent's Stone.

THE GOLDEN WHEEL

The Golden Wheel in Druidic cosmology refers to an interconnecting portal through which people could travel, even to the distant spheres of the galaxy. This fascinating concept is contained within the intricate geometry of this mandala. The pathway begins from the outer perimeter, Annwn (place of primal energy), goes into the trial of Abred (Earth) and ascends to the golden Circle of Gwynvyd, connecting ultimately with Ceugant, the cosmic home of the Creatrix. As a meditative glyph, it conjoins with unknown elements of the psyche bound in the Golden Wheel.

Anglo-Saxon brooch (9th century)

60

'FNIGMA OF THE BARDS'

'There is nothing truly hidden
But what is not conceivable.'

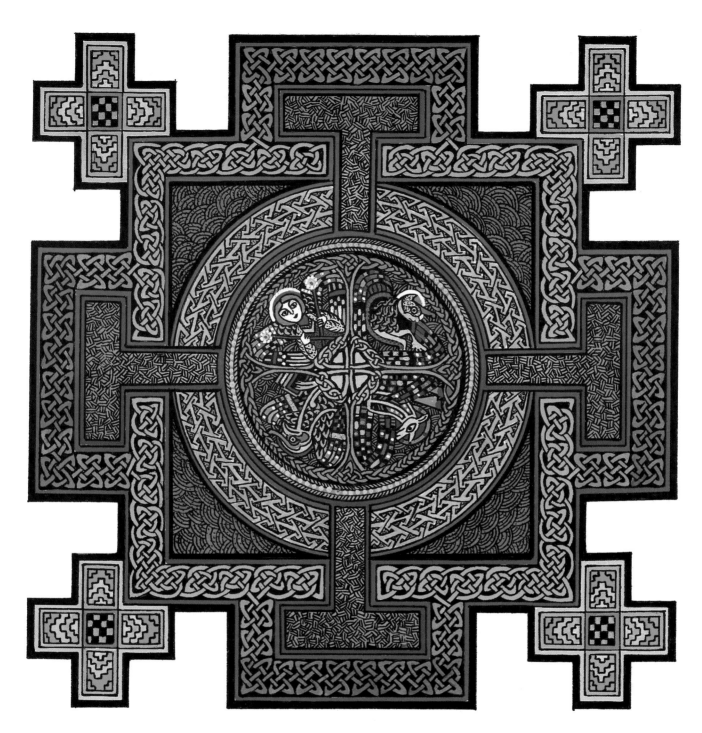

THE FOUR WINDS OF CREATION

Four is the primal number of the universe and the Druids identified the four elements of Creation – Water, Fire, Air and Earth – with the Four Winds of their invisible Creator. Such was the awesome power attributed to the elements by the Celts that it became the basis of a ritual oath-formula sworn by their warriors. As a meditative glyph, it endorses a sense of honour and courage. When life becomes a battlefield of despair or disillusion, evoke the Four Winds of Creation.

THE MIRROR OF CERIDWEN

The Mirror of Ceridwen reflects the image of the Great Lunar Goddess, whose penetrating gaze distils a sense of mystery. She has been referred to as the consort of Celi, the invisible Creator, but in earlier Celtic myths, Ceridwen was the Matriarchal Creatrix. This pathway may be most revealing for those seeking the feminine wisdom of the soul. As a meditative glyph, it dissolves rigid concepts that imprison the sensitivity of the psyche. When life becomes entrenched in dogma, evoke the Mirror of Ceridwen.

based on a 4th-century-BC inlaid disc.

based on an Anglo-Saxon brooch (9th century)

CONLA'S WELL

Conla's Well, whose source was the River Boyne, was in Irish myth the well of poetic vision; and the salmon found swimming there were believed to endow people with great wisdom or special gifts when caught and eaten. In another Irish myth, Tuan survives the Great Deluge which swept across Ireland by transforming himself into a salmon. The magical symbolism of this mandala reflects the mystical element of nature; the secret places humans seldom find, but visit in their dreams.

NIGHT OWL

The owl is an Earth creature who seeks the night, a solitary and silent bird of prey watching over a sleeping world. In Celtic myth, Blodeuwedd was transformed into an owl for having caused the death of Llew, a Sun king. Her fate or exile recalls the battle for supremacy between the solar and lunar deities. But the owl is considered a wise bird in all ancient folklore, wiser than the eagle — totem bird of Sun-kings. The magical symbolism of this mandala reflects this ancient lunar wisdom.

CELTIC HOROSCOPE

The passage of the planets or 'wandering stars' was keenly watched by the Druids, who drew up astral charts to record future auspicious events. They also drew up personal horoscopes – a practice referred to in the epic saga of Deirdre, when the Irish Druid Cathbad predicted a fateful future.

ARIES

A pentacle or five-pointed star forms the centre and is associated with Mars. The outer circle, a zoomorphic design of hunting birds, symbolizes the nature of warrior gods in Celtic myth. The astrological sign of Aries represents the vernal equinox, a significant turning point in the ritual Druidic calendar, when their Solar God reached manhood – an archetypal characteristic identified with the Alder God, Bran, and King Arthur. The hovering flight of the hawk on a windswept mountain creates a visual image of action and challenge.

TAURUS

A 'rose-hexagon', a six-sided crystal, reflects the lovely face of the Celtic Love Goddess Aine, associated with Venus. The outer circle of interconnecting spirals symbolizes the mystical feminine nature, which follows the invisible or instinctive thread of life. The soft outline contours of the land in Celtic myth represented the 'earthly form' of their Goddess and the crystal pools and rivers, her life blood. The chapel or sanctuary on the hill creates a visual image of the sacred spirit of all life.

GEMINI

The two curious semi-realistic human figures symbolize the Heavenly Twins, associated with Mercury and, in Celtic myth, with the Bardic God, Ogma. The Pictish key patterns surrounding the figures appear to place them in a labyrinth or maze. The role of Mercury or Ogma was to act as both teacher and guide into the inner planes or mysteries. Ogma also led departed souls safely through the Underworld during their journey on the Golden Wheel of Life – the Celtic belief in reincarnation. The visual image is therefore one of flux or alchemy.

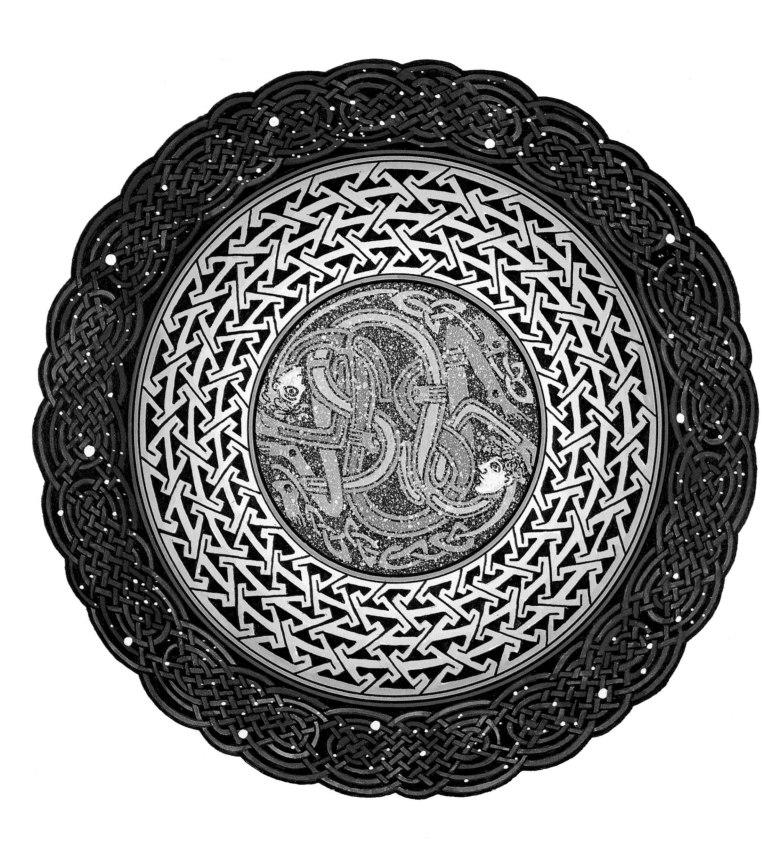

CANCER

The Moon is associated with this sign and is depicted as a silver disc divided into a crescent shape – a waxing and waning symbol. The zoomorphic design of hunting hounds surrounding the Moon recalls the ancient saga of 'the chase', which symbolized the changing light of the sky in both Celtic and Greek myth. Ceridwen, the Celtic Lunar Goddess, represented an ancient matriarchal source of wisdom and creation which was constantly challenged by invading continental tribes who had adopted a patriarchal system. The visual image reflects the eternal cycle of the Moon, which brings light and darkness in equal measure.

LEO

The Sun is associated with this sign and is symbolized by the four archangels or Gospels, which represented in the Book of Kells the Celts' conversion to Christianity and a patriarchal society. Jesus was identified with sacrificial sun gods and Ceridwen with the Virgin Mary. Her status, though somewhat diminished, was subtly restored in the Arthurian Graal legend. The stone dolmen signifies a portal into the realm of light or eternal life, which is the passageway of 'enlightened souls' in Celtic myth. The visual image is one of strength and self-sacrifice.

VIRGO

The veiled face of the Virgin holds two keys, symbolizing her role as Keeper of Secrets, which in Celtic myth provides access to both Heaven and Hell. Elaborate key patterns and key panels symbolize the discriminating nature of 'a veiled goddess', identified with Virgo. The Celtic Mercurial Goddess of Wisdom was Brigantia (Uranus), who acted as a guide into the inner mystery temple of visionary wisdom. The visual image reflects a 'puzzling' riddle or personal dilemma associated with the sign.

LIBRA

The royal figure of Guinevere, representing the autumnal equinox, holds the Scales of Justice, a traditional Libran symbol. She is guarding the entrance to Annwn, the fiery abyss or place of judgement in Celtic myth. The four swans symbolize the radiant beauty of the soul which is imprisoned and magically transformed at this time – the twilight zone. Arthur and Guinevere represent two important turning points in the solar year, growth and decay, which relate to personal growth astrologically. The visual image is therefore one of both joy and sorrow.

SCORPIO

Pwyll (Pluto), Lord of the Celtic Underworld, sits upon a huge crystal throne. His face is hidden, for he was the Dark Initiator, who guarded the four treasures of the Celts, which represented their superiority over all other races – symbols of power. These are depicted in the four surrounding knotwork panels: a sword and spear to defend their 'divine' right, and the chalice and stone (a crystal) to symbolize their belief in reincarnation and the immortality of the soul. Confronting Pwyll was part of this process – the visual image is one of 'realization', a transformation of the soul.

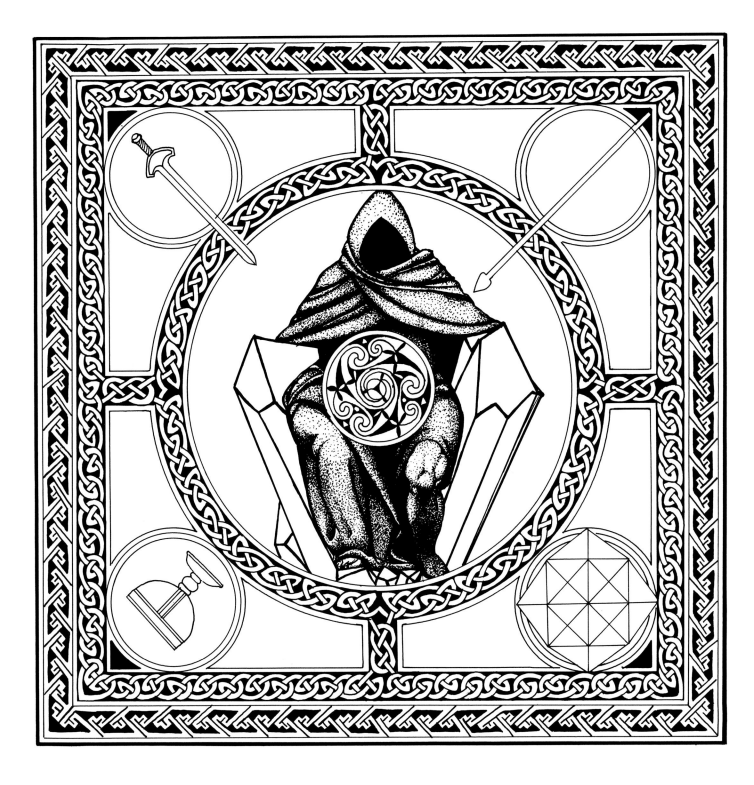

SAGITTARIUS

A centaur holding a bow and dispersing arrows far up into the sky is the traditional zodiac figure associated with Sagittarius. In Celtic myth their Horse Goddess was Epona or Rhiannon, an ancient matriarchal deity who represented their skill at horsemanship. Jupiter, the Greek Sky God associated with this sign, is identified with the Dagda, a father figure or patriarchal deity associated with the oak tree and the founder of the Druidic priesthood. This sign is related to 'higher' learning, so the visual image is one of freedom and self-exploration.

CAPRICORN

The ancient symbol of Saturn is a sea-goat, which is depicted as a goat scrambling up a steep precipice while its 'fish tail' is submerged in water. It represents the struggle of the soul in surmounting obstacles, which are often illusory. Saturn, or Sadorn in Celtic myth, is identified with Pryderi, the son of Rhiannon and Pwyll, who was abducted at birth. His disappearance caused an unjust penance for his mother, which relates to the hard lessons or karma associated with Saturn. The visual image reflects this difficult stage of spiritual metamorphosis.

AQUARIUS

Invisible hands reach out from behind clouds, holding two Celtic drinking cups, the contents being poured from one to the other. A jagged fork of lightning pierces the clouds and completes a scene of abstract symbolism which represents the visionary intelligence of Uranus. Brigantia or Brigid is associated with this planet and her Fire

Festival, celebrated on 1 February, symbolized the 'quickening' of the year, when the soul or spirit began spiralling out again from the darkness of winter. The visual image is one of healing light which inspires the hope and reconciliation of the New Age.

90

PISCES

Two large salmon swimming in a fast-flowing river are divided by a rainbow prism of light. One leaping fish heads upstream against the natural flow, while the other is content to remain in the shallow water of a rock pool, which symbolizes the duality aspect of the sign. The surrounding panels contain the zoomorphic figures of sea-horses and semi-realistic human shapes, which represent the 'shape-changing' realm of Neptune or the Celtic Sea God, Lir. The nature of Neptune and all sea gods is difficult to define, and the visual image reflects this intangible element of evolution – a mystical experience.

'THE ONE MYSTERY'

Evoke the ancient and the past
Will one illumining star arise?

J.C. Mangan

'THE QUEST'

They said: 'She dwelleth in some place apart,
Immortal Truth, within whose eyes
Who looks may find the secret of the skies
And healing for life's smart.'

James H. Cousins

further reading

MYTHOLOGY

Guerber, H.A. *The Myths of Greece and Rome*, Harrap, London, 1909

Rees, Alwyn and Brinley, *Celtic Heritage*, Thames & Hudson, London, 1989

Rolleston, T. W., *Myths and Legends of the Celtic Race*, Harrap, London, 1917

DRUIDISM

Nichols, Ross, *The Book of Druidry*, The Aquarian Press, Northampton, 1990

Spence, Lewis, *The Mysteries of Britain*, Society of Metaphysicians, 1986

POEMS AND VERSE

Marfell-Harris, Clare, *The Web of Enchantment*, In Letters of Gold, Cornwall, 1992

Monro, Harold, *Twentieth Century Poetry*, Chatto & Windus, London, 1929

Sharp, E. A. and J. Matthay, *Lyra Celtica*, John Grant, Edinburgh, 1932

For further information on the art of Courtney Davis write to:
3 Rodden Row, Abbotsbury, Dorset DT3 4JL,
enclosing 4 first-class stamps.

index